Brave Men of the Deep

A PART OF THE HISTORY OF SPRINGHILL'S MINING

HARRY E. MUNROE

authorHOUSE®

AuthorHouse™
1663 Liberty Drive
Bloomington, IN 47403
www.authorhouse.com
Phone: 1-800-839-8640

Published by AuthorHouse 12/01/2015

ISBN: 978-1-4969-5144-1 (sc)
ISBN: 978-1-4969-5143-4 (e)

Library of Congress Control Number: 2014919677

Print information available on the last page.

Contents

A Fourth Generation Coal Miner, Draegerman, And Rescue Worker During The Springhill Mine Disasters In 1956 & 1958.

These writings covers some of the interesting events that I remember during my years while working in the coal mines in Springhill and have listed them as follows:

1- The mine disasters and rescue operations from 1956-1958.
2- Poems about working in the coal mines which gives a walk through about a coal miner's experience as well as other poems that I have written.
3- The history of the Liars Bench and some of the stories that I have heard from those renowned gentlemen.
4- A history of Coal Mining in Springhill.
5- Springhill's connection with the Moose River Gold Mining disaster and rescue operations in 1936.

My Memories,
As a Miner and Draegerman,

During the Rescue operations at the Time of the 1956 and 1958 Mine Disasters in Springhill, N.S.

I was a fourth generation coal miner. My great grandfather, Henry Swift, was the underground manager at the time of what has been referred to as "the great explosion", on Feb. 21, 1891. He was among the one hundred and twenty-five men and boys who lost their lives.

My grandfather, Jim Davis, started working in the coal mines at thirteen years of age, and continued there for fifty-seven years, retiring at age seventy, He was almost blind by that time.

My father, Ira Munroe, worked a large part of his life in the coal mines. He worked at the coal face until he retired at the age of sixty-eight.

I started working in # 2 mine when I was sixteen years old, working on the 10-2 wall (10200 feet below ground). I went to night school, studying mining, and later other courses. I was also trained as a draegerman.

1956 started off as if it would be a normal year but trouble for the coal industry in Springhill was on the horizon. # 1 seam was close to depletion as no further development was being carried out, and the tunnel that was being driven from the 5700 foot bottom that was to open up #3 seam was halted.

I was one of the shot-fires on that project. The problem facing the coal industry, especially for Springhill, was that the major customer, C.N.R. was switching from burning coal to diesel.

#1 seam closed in the summer and the miners were transferred to # 2, but some left the area to seek other employment. I was transferred as a relief supervisor on the main slope of # 2 but I could see that coal mining was coming to an end so I was taking courses at night school and through correspondence to prepare me to enter into a different line of work.

One old timer that I worked with at that time, told me that I was wasting my time upgrading my education as in his words, there'll always be a coal mine in Springhill, but he lived to see that he was wrong.

A good number of miners that I had worked with in # 1 seam and were transferred to # 2 lost their lives in the 1958 bump. My being transferred to the position on the main slope of #2 no doubt saved me from being a casualty also.

In May, my wife's half brother, William (Manny) Whittle, was killed in the 13 800 east side long wall from a fall of roof stone.

On Thursday, November 1st, 1956, my wife and I were deer hunting on the Lewis meadow, approximately five miles from Springhill, when shortly after 5:00 PM we heard a loud explosion. At first I thought that one of the large boilers at the mine site had blown up. Then, hearing the steam whistle being blown, I realized that there was a problem at the mines, so we headed for home as quickly as possible.

When we drove into our yard, our neighbour was waiting to tell me that I was wanted at the mines as soon as possible. I grabbed a towel for showering, packed my wife and seven and a half year old son in the car, and headed for the mines. Cars were parked everywhere, so when I got to where McGee and Lower Cowan Streets intersect, I got out of the car and told my wife to drive over to Morris Street to her parents and stay there until I could get back to them – that turned out to be four days!

I proceeded down lower Cowan Street to the wash house to change from my street clothes to pit clothes, and then reported to the draeger house. Frank Stevens, who was normally in charge of the draegermen, was deer hunting up in the Westchester area at the time of the explosion. At that time, he had not arrived back at the mine site, so Lloyd Murray, who was a mine official, was passing out our breathing apparatus machines. (These were McCaa breathing machines that, when activated, were good for approximately two hours, according to the working conditions.)

The first crew that had arrived at the mine site was sent over to the main slope of #4, where the explosion had torn off the top part of the bank head. There they were instructed to go down to the first cross over, stopping between the airway (fan way) and the main slope to see if it was still intact. They were in line for the full force of the deadly gas. While only several hundred feet down in the slope, two of the draegermen collapsed.

I was among those sent in the second team to rescue our comrades. This was my first exposure to the devastation that the explosion had caused on the surface. When we got to the slope there was mass confusion with ones telling us not to touch this or that as it might crumble. When I first looked down the slope and saw Alex Spence and Benny Roy down – draegermen with many more years' experience than I, it made me wonder what chance I had if I went down to rescue them. However, I reflected on the training that Frank Stevens had given us, that is, to make sure that all the fittings on our machines were tight. Neil Ross, who was our team leader, put his hand on my shoulder and said, "We can do it, Harry!" So away we went, with a rope so that those on the surface could help pull the men up.

The first thing we did when we got to them was to make sure that their mouth piece was in place and the nose clip was on. (The equipment then did not have a face mask, but only a mouth piece, much like a scuba divers' outfit, and a nose clip.) We fastened the rope around them, one at a time, and placed them on their backs on the rail, balancing them as they were hauled to the surface. This method was used because the casing over the back of the breathing machine was metal so they slid along quite easily as those on the surface pulled on the rope. I cannot remember which of the two was brought to the surface first due to the confusion at that time, as well as the number of years since the event.

While we were busy down the slope, another tragic event took place. Bill Ferguson, another draegerman, came on the scene and had just stood at the entrance of the slope when he collapsed. By the time they got him over to the fresh air, he was dead.

Meanwhile, Alex Spence, one of the two draegermen we had brought up to the surface, was rushed to the All Saints Hospital, but was dead on arrival. Benny Roy was worked on by the mine nurses and they were able to revive him. Of those who went down the slope to bring these men up, at this time I can only remember Neil Ross, Hilton McNutt, and myself. We headed back to the draeger house feeling very discouraged, having lost two of our fellow draegermen, and as yet we had not even entered the mine to see if others might have survived the explosion.

By the time we had returned to the draeger house, Frank Stevens had arrived. He was a real team leader. He sat us down, explained what might have caused the loss of the two lives, and instilled in us the confidence we should have in the use of our breathing machines. We were also informed that other draeger crews were on their way from other mining communities to assist us.

I volunteered to go on the team that was to enter #4 mine through the explosion doors off #2 fanway at the 33 000 foot level, and go up into #4 main bottom. We were the first team to enter #4 and our team was made up of Vic Hunter, team captain, Amos Gogan, myself, and two others whose names I have forgotten. Our instructions were to survey the damage and to see if there were any signs of life in that area.

We went through two explosion doors up to the under tunnel, which was a tunnel under #4 main bottom, for an escape route in case there was a cave in on the main slope. As we came out on the back slope of #4, everything was deadly silent. We proceeded to where the back slope chain runner, Ephrain Alderson, was. He had been killed instantly from the force of the blast. We looked up the slope toward the hoisting engine, but due to a fall on the slope, we could not see Jack Ward, the hoisting engineer. (As a point of interest, Jack had traded shifts with Lee Blenkhorn on that particular day.)

We next proceeded toward the main slope. Halfway across the main bottom on the low side was a short tunnel housing a haulage engine for spotting the boxes (coal cars). We stopped to check this area. Gerald Dawson had been walking toward the haulage engine when the explosion occurred and he was lying face down, elbows outstretched. I remember grabbing him by one of his elbows, but he was now rigid. Burrel Pepperdine, who was operating the haulage was apparently first pushed back in his seat from the force of the explosion and then, as it passed, was pulled under the haulage drum. We then proceeded to the main bottom where we found the body of Lester Fisher. We neither had the time, nor were equipped, to recover their bodies at that time. There were fires burning on the main bottom from mine timbers, and the time period for our breathing machines was coming to an end, so we had to retreat from the area, return to the surface, and report our findings.

By this time, draeger crews from other mining areas had arrived to give us support. Next, the intention was to establish a fresh air station in the under tunnel of #4 by opening the explosion doors from #2 fanway slightly, to allow fresh air to enter and to save precious time for the dragermen as a place to rest. However, the fresh air entering the mine caused the fires to flare up, so our next task was to build stoppings around these areas to cut off the oxygen using brattice cloth (canvas impregnated with tar to make it air tight). This was then coated with a putty-like substance made from stone dust and water to make it fire retardant. A number of the draeger crews worked on this project. I worked with the team that had Raymond (Ray) Maddison as our captain. We were using copper hammers and nails for the building of these stoppings to prevent sparks, as the danger of another explosion was ever present. In talking to Kenneth Warren, who had worked in both #1 and #4 during the summers while going to college, I learned that he was one of the volunteers to assist in the rescue work. One of his tasks was mixing and carrying the putty for the stoppings being built.

On Saturday, before noon, some of the men from down in the deeps had made their way to the fresh air station. Charlie Burton and the others told of survivors, referring to Conrad Embree and the group under his leadership at the 5400 foot level.

A haulage hoist was set up on the auxiliary slope leading down to where Conrad Embree and his group were holed up. This took some time and then we had to wait for special oxygen cylinders and masks for those trapped men. The fear was that if they saw the rescue crews they would want to try and escape from their place of safety into the gas all around them, with the possibility that some would be lost. When everything was in place, we descended with a trolley to the 5400 with hot chocolate and coffee and the oxygen masks to rescue these ones. The last survivors were brought to the surface on Monday morning, November 5th.

Fearing another explosion, the mine was sealed with twenty-six bodies still remaining there. On January 19, 1957, the mine was reopened in order to recover those bodies. Number 4 was never opened again as a working mine. Tragically thirty-nine friends and fellow townsmen lost their lives in this disaster. There were many draegermen, bare faced miners, and other volunteers who deserve credit for their bravery and efforts to save their fellow men. The Canadian Liquid Air Company sent out letters to all the draegermen who participated in the rescue operation. As well, the story of the mine disaster was included in the December, 1956 issue of "Liquid Air Review", which I have included in this writing.

Canadian LIQUID AIR *Company*
Limited

KANE AND AGRICOLA STREETS
Halifax, N.S.

January 18, 1957.

Mr. Harry Munroe,
Springhill, N.S.

Dear Mr. Munroe:

As a tribute to the courage and
perseverance of those men who participated in the
rescue operations at the Springhill Mine last
November, our editors have included the story in
the current issue of the LIQUID AIR REVIEW.

We are pleased to send you herewith
a copy of this publication, as we understand from
Mr. H. C. M. Gordon you were one of the Draegermen
who took part in the rescue work. No doubt you
will find it of interest, particularly as it is
likely you will recognise some of the men in the
pictures.

We ask you to accept this copy of
the REVIEW as a remembrance of a job well done by
yourself and your fellow Draegermen.

Yours very truly,

CANADIAN LIQUID AIR CO., LIMITED.

G. C. ARTHEY
Manager

GCA/LAL.
Encl.

Dragermen emerging from surface buildings after completing a tour of underground duty at Springhill. Note the breathing tubes strapped to their chests. These connect their mouthpieces to the self-contained oxygen breathing apparatus carried on their backs.

"Greater Love Hath No Man..."

Maritime Mine Rescue Crews . . . Anonymous Canadian Heroes

UNTIL A FEW SHORT WEEKS AGO, the average Canadian had never even heard of "dragermen" or "bareface" miners. Who these men are, and what they do, was dramatically brought to every Canadian's attention during the first week of November 1956. At Springhill Nova Scotia, late in the afternoon of November 1st the normal way of life for that coal mining community was suddenly shattered by a devastating explosion in one of the town's two mines. The normal entrance to the mine was blocked and a furious fire was raging there as well. No one knew what conditions were underground, what had caused the explosion, or what fate had befallen the afternoon shift of miners working below.

The portable, closed circuit breathing apparatus on the back of a draegerman. Along the bottom is a small oxygen cylinder. Inside the casing are pressure reducing valves, a rubber breathing bag functioning as a low pressure oxygen reservoir, and a carbon dioxide absorbent for the exhaled breath.

Far underground were 118 trapped men . . . and into this picture immediately stepped the dragermen: carefully selected and highly trained volunteer miners, the shock troops of the coal mining industry. Working in rigidly disciplined teams of five men each, with their oxygen breathing equipment* strapped to their backs and masking their faces, they looked like men from another planet. With quiet courage the dragermen prepared to enter the mine. Ahead of them lay unknown dangers, which were to include blocked passages, an underground fire with accompanying dense smoke, and always the possibility of a second explosion. And above all, the most dreaded danger ---- the unseen, odourless, tasteless "after Damp" carbon monoxide loaded gas, produced by the incomplete combustion of the "fire damp", the methane gas which exists in most coal mines or coal dust.

The dragermen gradually worked their way down into the depths of the gas-filled mine, gaining entrance through a passageway connecting the shattered slope at the 3,300 ft. Level with an adjoining mine. Hour after hour in the search for their trapped fellow workers, the dragermen cleared passages, blocked off a fire and established "fresh air stations", by rebuilding stoppings in the cross-cuts to permit resumption of the normal air circulation in the mine which had been cut off by the explosion. At all times, they were protected against the carbon monoxide gas (1/10th of 1% can be fatal) by their oxygen breathing apparatus, yet at the same time, they were hampered by its weight and by the time limit ot imposed on how long they could work before returning to the surface.

Dicipline is the key word among draggermen; easch team carries rigid instructions from the mine rescue superintendent about the exact duties of his team and the time limit they are allowed to work. Dragger teams work in relays: for each team actually working underground, there is a releiving team statiooned at the underground fresh air base. Reserve teams wait on call at the surface, and as the working team is withdrawing (as their portable oxygen supply nears depletion), one of the teams on the surface is always on the way underground. The mine rescue superintendent accompanies the draggermen to the fresh air base, examines their equipment before they leave on their assignment, and remains on the spot until he is relieved. In this way, the draggermen's operations are always closely directed and supervised by a responsible mine official.

Meanwhile, above ground at Springhill relatives and friends gathered around the mine buildings waiting tensely for news. Large scale organizational operations were quickly established and coordinated to supply the requirements of the rescue crews and of an emergency hospital established to render prompt medical treatment to overcome rescue crew members and survivors. In a heartwarming spontaneous exhibition, assistance converged on Springhill from all over the Maritimes, and was offered from other parts of Canada and from the United States. Participating in this auxiliary work were the Canadian Legion, the Canadian Red Cross, the St. John's Ambulance Brigade, various church

organizations, the Salvation Army, the
R.C.M.P., the Navy, the Army, the Air Force
and over 50 doctors and 100 nurses who
volunteered their services.

About 30 men had been rescued relatively
early in the rescue operation, but then followed a long period of over 24 hours without
another survivor appearing. Then, after the
majority of the men had been trapped underground for 85 hours, the heroism of the mine
rescue workers backed by the efforts of the
supply organization, paid off in dramatic
fashion as the last 50 of the trapped men still
living were located at the 5,400 ft. level and
safely brought to the surface. Stories of indi-
vidual heroism, perseverance and of the high
sense of comradeship among the miners came
to light as fuller accounts of what actually
happened gradually emerged.

Of all the rescue equipment urgently needed
— and instantly provided — perhaps the
greatest necessity was for oxygen. Both underground and at regular and emergency hospitals established close by, oxygen was the
first and foremost requirement for treating
and reviving gassed men. An uninterrupted
supply of oxygen was also necessary to keep
the draegermen in action. Energetic steps
were therefore taken to ensure that there was
an abundant supply of oxygen at Springhill
throughout the period of rescue operations.
Large numbers of oxygen cylinders were immediately allocated and shipped from Maritime plants of Canadian Liquid Air Co. as the
main source of supply, but the R.C.A.F.
using small planes and 4 R.C.N. helicopters
airlifted cylinders from their Station at
Chatham, N.B., and hospitals in nearby cen-
tres also provided their supply. Even indus-
trial firms in the area offered their own stocks

of oxygen, so great was the desire to be of help.

But oxygen, life-sustaining though it may be, is only a commodity. It had to be transported down into the mine where it was needed by the teams of doctors underground. Every oxygen cylinder had to be carried individually by a man from the bottom of the operating "rake" (mine supply train) at the 3,300 ft. level, along a horizontal passageway — a distance of 2,200 ft. — to the fresh air base. Standard, large size oxygen cylinders were too heavy to be transported in this way, especially under the existing hazardous conditions. Small cylinders were therefore needed in great quantity. Medical type oxygen cylinders, normally used in hospitals for attachment to oxygen tents and anaesthetic machines were of considerable value for resuscitators. In even greater demand was another type of cylinder used by the R.C.A.F. for high altitude flying. These are so-called "drop bottles", equipped with their own pressure reducing regulators and breathing masks, and were ideal for transport and use underground. The R.C.A.F. supplied hundreds of them.

As the dragermen, bareface miners and teams of doctors (most of whom had not been inside a mine before) were moving in and out of the mine during the long, anxious hours of the rescue operation, one of the main tasks was the constant shuttling of the samll oxygen cyliunders back and forth from the surface, where each cylinder (including the dragermen's) was instantly refilled under close supervisiobn from banks of large cylinders established there. When rescue operations neared their climax, there were at any time as many as 90-100 men underground. The oxygen was of great value down in the mine for on-the-spot use by the doctors. Whenever a bareface miner was overcome from too long exposure to the carbon monoxide in the ventilating air, he was immediately given oxygen treatment. Many of the bareface miners carried an oxygen cylinder along with them as they worked, as a precautionary measure. The presence of the doctors underground, with their oxygen therapy equipment, speeded the recovery of overcome men, and in some cases undoubtly saved their lives. (Later on, oxygen was administered in the same way to any of the survivors poisoned by carbon-monoxide, as they passed through on their way to the surface). In their determination to work as long as they could underground to aid their trapped comrades, the bareface men would disregard their personal safety. On more than one occasion, some even had to be ordered out of the mine, when extreme physical exertion or exposure to carbon monoxide had weakened their resistance.

Throught all these supporting operations the draggermen continued their dangerous duties, probing deeper and deeper in the mine. Finally, three of the trapped miners bravely and unselfishly made their own way up through gas-filled passages from the 5,400 ft level, to report that 50 of their fellow workers were waiting there for rescue, sustaininbg their lives by sucking air from punctures in a compressed air line used to supply machinery. Rescue operations then reached a peak in urgency.

Many hours before this the dragermen had sealed off a severe undergrounnd fire. This fire was located just beyond the fresh air base, and the smoke and carbon-monoxide gas that resulted made it necessary to curtail the amount of air admitted to the mine. In spite of all efforts, the fire continued to burn and led to an extremely dangerous situation when the trapped men were located. Ventilation had to be increased along the path the trapped men would travel from the 5,400 ft level to the surfac, and yet the air supply had to be minimized in the fire area, to prevent a swecond explosion at a time when there were so many men in the mine.

Speaking afterwards of the mine rescue crews, Mr. Harold Gordon, Vice-President and General Manager of the Dominion Coal Company, who personally directed rescue operations and was underground 90% of the time, and himself a former drageman, said:"Men worked under the most terrifying and difficult conditions. I know of no man who did not do his utmost, and most of them went far beyond the call of duty. It wasa marvelous performance under the most difficult circumstances. In the conditions which existed underground aftefr the explosion, the fact that any man survived is nothing short of a miracle. Eighty-eight were brought to the surface alive."

With all the living men successfully evacuated, the mine had then to be sealed because of the imminent danger of a second explosion. Springhill's joy at the escape of the 88 men was tempered by sadness, for in all 39 men lost their lives as a result of the explosion.

Throughout all the operations at Springhill, one picture stands out in sharp relief --- the indimitable courage of the dragermen and bareface miners, and their willingness to perform their incredibly hazardous duties out of a high sense of duty to their trapped fellow miners, and without any thought of praise or monetary gain. This feeling of brotherhood and comradship among the coal miners of the Maritimes is underlined by the fact that the dragermen at Springhill were not entirely drawn from the local miners. Dragermen came as well from other Nova Scotian mining centers in Pictou County and Cape Breton Island. These drager teams worked just as hard, undertook the same risks in the same spirit of self-sacrifice as did the dragermen from Springhill itself.

The names of the mine rescue workers are not known to us, especially to those of us living in central and western Canada, but what they did is indelibly printed in our memories. Dragermen do not expect attention or praise for the long hours of training they voluntarily undergo to prepare themselves for their dangerous work, nor for what they do when mining accidents occur. It took a disasterr, such as Springhill, to make us even aware of their existence. Surely in this hurried, too often cynical world, the Maritime dragermen and bareface rescue crews are living proof of the oft-quoted but seldom practised Christian docturne that "Greater love hath no man for his friewnds". Both the dragermen and the bareface rescue workers risked their lives every minute they worked underground: two of the dragermen actually gave their lives. In realization of the quiet heroism of these anonymous miners, Canadian LiquidAir Company humbly pays them unqualified tribute. We will long remenber them.

Draegermen being fitted with their oxygen breathing equipment before entering mine.

In the cold light of dawn, Mr. Harold Gordon (right), who supervised rescue operations, makes one of his brief appearances at the surface.

MARITIME RESCUE CONTINUED

Above: An R.C.N. helicopter, just after landing at Springhill with a supply of small size oxygen cylinders. Helicopters were also used to evacuate seriously overcome miners to hospitals in Halifax.

Another team of the courageous draegermen wait outside the mine rescue station for their turn in the relay relief of teams working underground.

Some of the Springhill Draegermen during the 1956 Explosion

Some of the Springhill Draegermen during the 1956 Explosion

The Author Harry Munroe

1957 seemed to be a normal year, with the #4 explosion behind the town for approximately one year, when on Dec. 26, 1957, a fire broke out in Stedman's store on main street. It was discovered at Approximately 10:30 PM. High winds fanned the flames. I was working on the main slope of #2 mine as the relief supervisor on the 11 PM to 7 AM shift. When the work crew and I came to the bank head (surface) at 3 AM, as we looked toward Main Street it appeared that the whole business section of the town was on fire. The Springhill fire department, as well as fire departments from other areas rushed in to assist, had it under control by the next morning. The extent of the damage was clearly visible- fourteen businesses and four private homes had been destroyed. It was another major blow to the coal mining town.

By the start of 1958, with the closures of #1 and #4 mines, the work force had been reduced, and many of the businesses that were destroyed in the 1957 fire did not rebuild, so these events were now bringing about changes to the town's prosperity.

When I first started working in the #2 mine, I had been assigned to work in the long walls, these were 400 feet long. When you would get a "bump" things would shake. The pressure following these would cause the packs and timbers to creak and groan. Then things would start to settle and the air would be full of coal dust for a few minutes before clearing, then everyone would go back to work. These "bumps" occurred as the coal was being mined and the open space allowed the floor of the mine to push up with extreme pressure, much like an earthquake.

On April 18, 1958 a fire started on the west side of the back slope #2, at the 13800 ft. level, between the air slope and the back slope. A tugger rope, which was in use, was chaffing against some overhead timbers, thus starting the fire. I was part of the draeger crew dispatched to the area. We built a temporary stopping (barrier) on the air slope side of the fire to cut off the oxygen while we prepared to lay a water pipe line from a water sump some 800 feet up the slope from us. Thus we had the fire contained between the two stoppings. If we could not get the fire out that would have been the end of the #2 mine.

It took several hours to lay the pipeline and prepare the hoses, leaving the fire to smolder for some time. When everything was ready, the stopping on the air slope was opened, and when the air hit the smoldering fire, it took off with a roar, sounding like a blow torch, but we were able to bring it under control with the water hoses.

A letter of commendation was sent from the Department of Mines concerning this incident to all those involved. My copy is enclosed.

File No. ....

DEPARTMENT OF MINES
PROVINCE OF NOVA SCOTIA

Halifax, April 30, 1958.

Mr. Harry Munroe,
Springhill,
Nova Scotia.

Dear Mr. Munroe:

  The fire which started in No. 2 Colliery on April 18th, 1958, could have brought disaster to the mine with its repercussions on the Town of Springhill.

  You are to be commended for your decision to enter the mine in the face of imminent danger to attempt to wall off and put out the fire.

  I wish to thank you for your brave action and to congratulate you on its successful conclusion.

Yours very truly,

E. A. Manson,
Minister of Mines.

On Thursday, Oct. 23, 1958, shortly after 8 PM, disaster struck. The shock wave from the "bump" was felt throughout Springhill, rattling dishes on the shelves, cracking some foundations of houses etc. The shock wave registered on the seismographs in Halifax's Dalhousie University, approximately 100 miles away.

I was at my father-in-law's home on Morris Street, about one-third mile away from the mine site and it literally shook the house. Fully aware of what had happened, I rushed to the mine, got into my pit clothes, and reported to the draeger house just as some who had survived the "bump" were reaching the surface with stories of the damage.

The "bump" had released a tremendous amount of dust and methane gas, making things extremely dangerous. It had also affected the ventilation system which normally cleared the air. The draeger team I was with went in at the 13400 foot level, almost to the coal loader machine, but the way was blocked from there. On our side of the loader we found three men trapped on the low side of the level. The "bump" had pushed the floor of the level up to the point that they had only about a foot of space from their heads to the roof. All three had crushed vertebras in their backs from the impact of the "bump" under their feet, and if it had not been for the space above their heads, it probably would have broken their necks.

With the fallen debris around them, and because they were buried up to their shoulders, it made for very tight working conditions to rescue them. We had to work on our knees, and used basket type stretchers with runners on them to get them out. These three were Jack Scott from Clairmont, Kenneth Gilbert from Upper Cowan Street, and a fellow worker whose last name was Wilson.

Once the ventilation system was repaired and the mine was cleared of methane gas, the draegermen were no longer required as the rescue work was now being carried out by bare faced miners. I then volunteered to work as a bare faced miner in the rescue work and recovery of the bodies. These were identified by the number on their lamp battery. The bodies were carefully wrapped in plastic sheets and blankets and placed in metal coffins with an air-tight seal at the top. These metal coffins were designed to fit inside a regular casket.

To complete this rescue operation would take 14 days with several highs and lows as the rescue workers pressed on in the hopes that some had survived the bump and was awaiting rescue.

On Sat. Oct. 25th. General Manager Harold Gordon held a press conference expressing his feelings after surveying the underground workings, that there was little or no hope of any survivors. Still the rescue workers pressed on under very difficult conditions, and on Thurs. Oct. 30 they were rewarded for their efforts when 12 were found alive.

This in turn spurred on the rescue workers in their hopes that yet more may have survived the bump and still be alive.

The following day Mr. Harold Gordon held another press conference stating that he could not see how any more could have survived due to the passing of time. Again he was wrong.

Several days later, on Nov. 1st. another 7 survivors were rescued and brought to the surface.

The first to be found was Barney Martin who was a distance below where the other 6 was found. He was in a narrow place between two packs with only enough space to get up on his knees and not able to get himself out without help, so he spent all that time in isolation.

The other 6 were in a group and encouraged one another not to loose hope.

On Thursday, Nov. 6th. 14 days after the ordeal had begun, the last of the Bodies was removed from the mines, this was in fulfillment of the miners unwritten code, that regardless of how long it take, they would come and rescue or recover their fellow workers.

I worked with the rescue crews until the last bodies were brought to the surface.

100 miners had been rescued, 74 died in the bump, and 1 died later from his injuries, bringing the total who lost their lives to 75.

Following this, a salvaging operation took place for the equipment that could be put to use in other Dosco's operations, and in July, 1959, #2 mine was sealed. This brought to an end Dosco's mining operations in Springhill. On Nov. 16TH. 1959, the Carnegie Hero Fund Commission awarded a Gold Medal and Bronze Plaque to the Heroes of the Springhill Mine Disaster. My copy of the invitation is enclosed.

Springhill, N. S.
November 16, 1959.

Dear Sir:

The Carnegie Hero Fund Commission has awarded a Gold Medal and Bronze Plaque to Heroes of Springhill Disaster 1958 and presentation will be made by Premier Stanfield at the Capitol Theatre, Springhill, Nova Scotia, November 25, 1959, at 3:30 p.m. The Award is to a group of which you are one.

The Springhill Committee on Arrangements would like every man sharing the Award to wear the ribbon of identification on November 25th. The Ribbon is a memento of the Award, given only to men who risked their lives in rescue work underground October 23 - November 2, 1958. We trust all who possibly can will attend the Presentation on November 25th.

In order to have your group seated together, the side door of the Theatre will be open for Awardees only from 2:40 p.m. until 3:15 p.m. The public entrance will open at 3:10 p.m.

The Committee has arranged a reception in your honour at the Legion Hall immediately following the Presentation and trusts you and your wife, or next of kin, will attend.

Yours sincerely,

Stephen T. Pyke
Chairman,
Springhill Committee

Strange as it may seem to some people, I would have to say that I enjoyed my years working in the coal mines as I found that every day the working conditions were different and challenging. The comradery that developed with fellow workers has left me with many fond memories.

In keeping with my coal mining experience, I have written a number of poems which give an overview of the life of a coal miner. (The words to these are included.)

1. "The Lamp Cabin Story" (When reporting for work after changing into your pit clothes, you go to the lamp cabin for your light.)
2. "Story Time in the Pest House" (This was located under the mine bank head. There were benches to sit on while waiting to enter the mine. There you filled your water can and it became a great place for the story tellers while waiting.)
3. "Riding the Trolleys" (It was the means of taking you to the mines.)
4. "A Coal Miner's Life" (This gives an overview of what could be described as a "normal life" of a coal miner.)
5. "Working on the 10-2 Wall" (This was my first experience when starting out as a coal mine worker.)
6. "The Long Wall Fattening Stall" (While the men working on the long wall were all on the same tally, some did not do their share of the work.)
7. "The Coal Miners' Wash House Blues" (After a hard day's work in the mines you would then return to the surface and head for the showers in the wash house, but the water was not always hot.)

I have also written several songs about the coal mining way of life – "The Town Called Springhill" about the mine disasters and the rescue operations, and "Brave Men of the Deep", describing the type of men

who worked in the mines at Springhill. I have recorded these songs and poems on a CD entitled "Brave Men of the Deep".

I have taken the time to write this information at the urging of my family and friends. As these were events that have happened in the distant past, they may soon be forgotten by future generations.

Harry E. Munroe

The Lamp Cabin Story

1- To help the miners down deep in the mines
They must have a lamp that will really shine
To light up the roadway and the long wall
And help them timber the roof so it won't fall.

2- So from the wash house to the lamp cabin they must go
And to pick up their lamp a check number they must show
To indicate that they were entering into the deep
And the boys in the lamp cabin their talley they would keep.

3- Now those lamp cabin boys were humorously inclined
And sometimes tell you a story if you had the time
There was Ralph, Alf, Harry and Jim
They were men that the miners had confidence in.

4- And when the miners came up out of the mines
For the lamp cabin they would make a bee- line
To turn in their lamp and pick up their check
From one of the boys that they had come to respect.

5- So the lamp cabin was just another part
Of a coal miners life from the very start
And though those boys never entered the mines
They provided the needed light with a lamp that would shine.

Story Time IN The Pest House

1- Under the bankhead and in the pest house of # 2
There's a story going around that just can't be true
So some would listen intently while others they'd talk
But to some of the stories you can't take much stalk.

2- There some would tell of their aches and pains
While others would tell of their stress and strains
They all seemed to promote some miracle cure
That they had bought at the local drugstore.

3- Sometimes their stories were in serial form
Just like the soap operas that are now the norm
Some would just sit and chew and spit
While others would demonstrate their humor and wit.

4- My father would leave home shortly after lunch
To hear the full story from that story telling bunch
And each one would add a line or two
Until they really believed that the stories were true.

5- I learned through the years not to doubt these wise men
Because a long life of experience they could transcend
So the younger ones would quietly show their respect
To the long winded stories that they could expect.

Riding The Trolleys

1- To enter the mines by the trolleys you must go
But to some they seemed to travel so slow
Especially when they were on their way home
So some would sit, complain and moan.

2- And some when they were entering into the deep
Would sit in the trolleys and go to sleep
While others were anxious to reach the incline
So that the coal they could mine.

3- Sometimes the trolleys would give a jerk
As the men were being lowered down to work
Some from fear their chewing they would swallow
While others would just sit there and holler.

4- The top seat in the trolleys was considered the best
Because while riding they could lay back and rest
While in the rest of the seats you were cramped and squeezed
As the ones in front of you would lay back at ease.

5- So if you ever go into a mine
Don't forget to keep this in mind
Make for the top seat in the trolleys to ride
Then your trip will be pleasant with comfort on your side.

A Coal Miners Life

1- My dad was a coal miner, and my grand-dad too
They worked their whole lives down in old #2
Their lives they spent working from daylight till dark
So their families they could feed, and give them a start.

2- A coal miners life was hard at it's best
As deep underground the work gave no rest
The dust they would breathe deep into their lungs
So old men they were while they were yet young.

3- They worked in dangers, explosions and bumps
To mine the coal our economy to pump
For coal reigned as king during that era of time
And many a young man would enter the mine.

4- I starter working under-ground at 16 yrs. of age
As being a coal miner was then the rage
To do my best I was determined to try
Although many friends you would see die

5- And also there was the story tellers so fine
So on the liars bench they would pass the time
As each one by story they would try to out-do
The things that had happened in old # 2.

6- So this my friends you can be sure
These brave men of the deep were really mature
They were buddies to me at an important time
So I'll always remember them as friends of mine.

Working On The 10-2 Wall
(10200 Longwall)

1- When just a young lad of 16 years
From working in the coal mines I had no fear
I was assigned to work in the 10-2
I'm telling you that was quite a crew.

2- To Red Bob Smith I would report
He was a man that could get out of sorts
I was assigned 2nd man on the packs
And you had very little time to relax.

3- Now as you would travel up the long wall
Then to each miner you would call
To see if they were ready for you to build a pack
That would hold up the roof over their backs.

4- Now there was Percy Tabor, Ray and Dick
Of them Percy Was the one to use the pick
While Ray and Dick would shovel the coal
As down the shaker pans it would roll.

5- The rest of the miners of that longwall crew
Worked the buddy system that they best knew
Because their safety depended upon each other
So to each one they became just like a brother.

6- Once in awhile you'd get a bump
Sometimes it would really make you jump
But after the coal dust it would clear
Then you would put behind any fear.

The Long Wall Fattening Stalls

1- Of the 30 men working on the long wall
You always had one or two fattening stalls
These were men who worked at the coal face
But with the other men they never kept pace.

2- The men of the long-wall had their tally
So the number of loaded boxes was their rally
As well as the timber that they would install
It helped boost the pay of the men on the long wall.

3- Sometimes they would be paid for shoveling out
Or the hard bench that they had to jack-hammer out
To get the wall ready for a shift of the pans
Which was carried out by the company-hands.

4- It made no difference if the coal was close or far away
Those in the fattening stalls never really earned their pay
So as they dallied their time on the long wall
Their work place was referred to as a fattening stall.

The Coal Miner's Wash House Blues

1- You come out of the mines covered with grime and dirt
And you head for the wash-house to take off your shirt
You go to the shower so brave and bold
And turn on the water only to find that it's cold.

2- And the air outside it's chilly and cold
So to take a shower one must be bold
But shower you must in order to be clean
But the boilers can't supply all the steam.

3- Sometimes the water it might be hot
But most of the time it's really not
So you go under the shower with the greatest of ease
And hold your breath as you try not to freeze.

4- So the washout blues you can never forget
And how your buddies would frown and fret
But of one thing you could be sure
When you'd come out of the showers, someone would open the door.

5- So a cold blast of air you were sure to get
That's why the wash-house blues we'll never forget
But after all it was a way of life
So we'll always remember it for the rest of our life.

In the heart of Springhill stands this stone and marble monument, topped by the figure of a miner. It commemorates the 125 men who lost their lives in the town's first mining disaster,

The Miner's Monument was first erected in memory of the 125 men and boys killed in the 1891 explosion. It was first located on upper main street on the lot above the former Dr. Murray property and was unveiled on Sept. 11-1894. In Bertha Scott's book she refers to it as the white miner.

It was moved to it's present location after the Miner's Hall was built in 1927. (Now the Library) Besides the original names of the 1891 miners, the monument mow has stone plaques containing the names of all those who lost their lives in the 1956 explosion; 1958 bump and all others during the 80 years of mining in Springhill, for a total of over 430 brave miner.

The following is a sample of some of the other poems that I have written over the years:

This one I wrote after an article appeared in the Springhill Record about a beaver being sighted in the parking lot at Tim Hortons.

The Day The Beaver Visited Tim Hortons

1- There's a story going around
   And they say that it's true
   Of a beaver visiting Tim Hortons
   To check out their brew.

2- We humans are a curious cuss
   So the beaver decided to visit us
   To see if the stories are really true
   Of how Springhiller's like their Tim Hortons brew

3- Now I'm not a doubter, you can agree
   So I'll tell the story as it was told to me
   And the Springhill Record say's it's so
   So off to Tim Hortons you should go.

4- That's why all the folks gather around
   To the Tim Hortons that's in our town
   So if even beavers like their brew
   Then it should be good for me and you.

Harry Munroe

Our Home Town Girl

1. There is a girl from our home town
    Who has gained international renown
    Because she has a beautiful singing voice
    And has made many a heart rejoice.

2. She started out with the Sing Along Jubilee
    And they aired the show on the C.B.C.
    It was form this humble start
    That she has won the peoples hearts.

3. Then there was the Snow Bird song
    It was a tune that did catch on
    And brought Anne into international fame
    So she became a household name.

4. She also has her many awards
    Which has struck a happy Chord
    From Grammy's Oscar's and all the rest
    To the home town folks she is the best

5. So if you visit our friendly town
    You'll see the people as they gather around
    For a visit to the Anne Murray Center they come
    To learn about Anne and the things she'd done.

By - Harry E. Munroe

Harry, Thank you.

Anne Murray 2002

The Wintertime Blues

1- The snow it keeps falling
    And the weatherman keeps calling
    For no let up in the storm
    While I sit here wishing
    It was time to go fishing
    Or go someplace where it's warm.

2- I checked with my neighbour
    And knew it would take labour
    To get the car out of the yard
    But with it still snowing
    I know I'm not going
    Very far with it storming so hard.

3- I think I'll go skiing
    Then It's like being
    Somewhere that has hills and vales
    So I'll be pretending
    That spring is just ending
    And summer is just over the dale.

4- It's no good to worry
    Because you can't hurry
    The wintertime blues away
    So I'll just take it easy
    And stay where it's breezy
    And wait for the month of May.

    By Harry Munroe

My Martin Guitar

I am the proud owner of a Martin Guitar
It's a brand name that's known both wide and far
And because of their quality and sound
For many years they have been around.

Mr. C. F. Martin began in 1833
To make guitars for both you and me
They are hand-crafted with the greatest of care
And have a quality that is beyond compare.

I learned to play at an early age
As country music was then the rage
And you needed a guitar that would carry the sound
So that it could be heard all around.

So when I go to a party or jamboree
My Martin Guitar is always with me
And whether they are a friend or guest
They recognize my Martin as one of the best.

For a company that has such a fine reputation
May it continue on to the next generation
To produce guitars with the same quality and sound
Which will guarantee that they will still be around.

Harry Munroe

The Story Of The Liars Bench
(Author sitting on the bench.)

The Liars Bench is situated on the corner of McGee street and Lower Herrett road. The lower Herrett road had a row of Coal company houses on both sides. These were double houses with two families per house that had been built by the coal company for the miners and their families and was in close walking distance to the coal mines.

The liars bench was built by the miners as a place to congregate during their leisure time and tell their stories as a form of entertainment. When the miners were afternoon shift (3pm. To 11 pm.) they would congregate in the morning until noon, then go home for dinner and prepare to go to work. The miners on day shift (7am. To 3 pm.) would gather on the liars bench after they had supper on into the evening and sometimes in the cooler weather they would build a bonfire to keep themselves warm.

One day while the miners was working their wives got together and painted the words "The Liars Bench.", on it. Needless to say, the miners were not happy with the designation as they often claimed that their stories were real life experiences, while trying to outdo one another.

For years it became a tourist attraction as many would stop and talk to the miners and be amazed at their wisdom. At one time they had a log book so people could sign their names in it. One famous person who had stopped to talk to the miners and sign the log book was Jack Dempsey who was on his way to Halifax to referee a wrestling match and as the story goes, he was so taken up with the miners stories that he was almost late for the wrestling match. Sad to say, that log book has disappeared but the Liars Bench is still part of Springhill's famous history that should be cherished.

The following are some of the stories that I have heard:

When # 4 mine was opened in the late 1930's, the mine management brought a man from Cape Breton for manager. His name was Donald MacLeod who was short and squatty, and Springhiller's who were noted for giving people nick names, called him Donald Duck, or the Duck which he accepted with humor.

Now, Earl McCarthy, who was the fan-way Chain runner, in his early years boxed under the name of kid McCarthy, and when you think of the word kid, he was nicknamed the goat, and the really got his goat, ba-a ing at him when he was not looking, so one day he went in to manager Donald MacLeod's office (the Duck's), to complain about what was happening. Manager MacLeod, (the duck) humerous as he was, said to Earl McCarthy, (the goat), Earl, I'll trade my feathers for your horns any time you want to. Needles to say, that did not go over very well with the goat.

On another occasion, on a nice sunny afternoon, a group of us was gathered around the fan-way slope, waiting to go down the mines, and having some idle time on our hands, a plane high up in the sky was passing by and Earl McCarthy said I wouldn't want to be up there in that (referring to the plane) and Kenny Ross the hoisting engineer for the fan-way responded, Earl, I wouldn't want to be up there without it.

Another time, again while waiting to go down into the mines, Earl McCarthy was telling us that he had a relative die in the United States and had the body sent home by air freight, but he thought that the price was awful expensive, so Kenny Ross said to Earl, do you know why it cost so much? It was dead weight.

On another humerous note, one spring day when people were starting to get their cars out from winter storage Earl took his car up to Cecil Letcher's garage on main street, and was letting the air out of his tires, as they had an outside air hose and gauge there. Cecil noting what Earl was doing came out from his office to see if he was having trouble with his tires so Earl started to explain to him how the air in your tires gets stale and should be changed every year. Apparently this was a new thought for Cecil Letcher.

Another interesting person to listen to was Clarence Pepperdine. At the end of the second world war Model 'A' Cars were highly sought after and Clarence was the proud owner of one. In those days the majority of the roads were not snow plowed out so those with cars patiently waited for spring to go Sunday driving and Clarence was no exception. Now Clarence's wife Lucey was on the heavy side so to make sure that the Spring weight restrictions had been lifted he called Corporal Bill Tayler of the R.C.M.P. to get the ok in order to take Lucey for a drive.

Now Clarence worked as a chain runner on the bank head of #2 main slope which required unhooking the chain of the rake of coal as it was coming up out of the mine. The rake of coal consisted of 16 boxes of coal with a combined weight of approximately 32 tons. The hoisting rope was a 1-3/4 inch steel cable, a socket and three large links. The socket and three links weighed 100 lbs., and as the rake was coming up out of the mines Clarence would put his left hand on the top of the front box and run backwards with the rake until it was over the brow of the slope and the rake would run forward enough to slacken off the chain so he could unhook it with his right hand. Because of the awkward position he was lifting in Clarence developed the piles so Clarence inquired from some of the old timers (considered the wise men) what would be good to cure his piles and was told to use slones liniment, so on his way home from work he stopped at the local drugstore and obtained a bottle.

According to Clarence, after supper he went to his outside toilet, and being a little nervous of how he would react to it, dropped his drawers and put just a little dab on the ends of his fingers on his right hand in order to give the piles a little pat. When he did so according to Clarence, the cheeks of his behind come together so fast that it black & blued all the fingers on that hand. He never did say if it cured his piles.

On another occasion Clarence came to work on a Monday looking tired and hung over. Now Clarence lived on Pine street which runs pair-ell with the Junction Road which is the main road to the middle of the town and has a slope of about 30 degrees. So when ask why he was so tired he said that he had been drinking dog berry wine all day Saturday and ended up chasing cars up and down the Junction road on Sunday which wore him out.

Percy Tabor was another interesting person to listen to. In fact he sat on the top position on the liar's bench. When I first started working in #2 mine on the 10,200 long wall Percy Tabor, was a miner who worked close to the top on that wall and I might add that the long wall was 400 ft. long, so when coal production was at a standstill while waiting for coal boxes us young ones would gather around Percy to listen to his stories.

One Friday Percy was telling us young ones that he was going to go fishing on the weekend so we said among ourselves that we were in for a dandy fish story when he came back to work on Monday.

When we returned to work on Monday we were anxiously waiting to hear his story but he wasn't saying anything so curiosity got the best of us and when we had the chance we ask Percy about his fishing trip, expecting him to tell us about the big one that got away. Instead he said that he was all done fishing, and that he was not going fishing anymore. So naturally we ask if it was because the big one got away? His reply was no, but the fish he caught were so small that he had to take them to the jeweler to get them cleaned.

He claimed that this was a true life experience.

This is another amazing story as told by Jim Brennan and Frank Brown to a group of us young ones while working in the mines. It was about a granite rock weighing about ½ ton in the crotch of a maple tree about 20 ft. in the air up in Lynn mountain. Under normal circumstances you might find this story hard to believe but when the story is substantiated by a witness then you have to accept it as true.

Their theory was that a maple seed had gotten deposited under this rock and when it started to grow it just started to push this rock up with it to the position that it is in today. In this case Frank Brown came to his support. When Jim Brennan was telling the story he said to Frank, isn't that right Frank? His reply was, that's right Jimmie, I've seen it dozens of times. Now I'm not a doubter, but I have a hunting camp on Lynn mountain and have travelled that woods for over 50 years and have not as yet came across this tree with the huge granite boulder in it's crutch. But on the other hand, how could you doubt these wise old gentlemen even though it is an amazing story.

The Story Of The Cow That Swallowed The Turnip:

This story took place on the Canning farm in the early thirties on the Athol road. The story was told to me by both the Canning brothers, Ron and Ken on two occasions and as they say, that out of the mouth of two witnesses it must be true. Their father was killed in a car accident and in those days there was no widow's allowance so the boys were trying to help their mother run the farm. In those days some farms were raising cattle turnips as a supplement with hay to feed the cattle. Some farms had a turnip pulper to cut up the turnips to make it easier for the cattle to eat them but the Canning's could not afford one so they would try to cut them up by hand.

On this particular day one of the cows tried to swallow a turnip whole and it got stuck in its throat and started to choke from the lack of air. At that time Ron was 12 yrs. Old and Ken was 10 yrs. Old. The boys didn't know what to do and was afraid of loosing the cow so one of them ran up to Frank Stonehouse's farm which was about ¼ mile away for help.

Now Frank Stonehouse was a big barrel chest-ed man who reminded you of a lumber jack and he ran a farm as well as lumbering, so he went with the boy to the canning farm, sized up the situation, and told the boys to get a piece of plank about 3 ft. long and the fence mall and then he was ready for action. Ken who was the youngest was told to hold the cows tail off to one side and Ron was to hold the plank against the cows rectum and when all was in place Frank Stonehouse with the fence mall in his hand belted the cow on the rectum and according to the Canning boys the turnip flew out of the cows mouth and hit the side of the barn just like it had been shot out of a cannon, so the cow survived the ordeal.

You can see the truthfulness of this because when a child tries to swallow something and starts to choke the first thing they used to do was hit it on the bottom. All these individuals have now passed away but I knew Ron and Ken for many years.

Red Gallagher's Coon Dog: One day a group of miners got into a discussion about their dogs and how smart they were. One had a dog that could stand up and walk on his hind legs just like a person. Another had a dog that could jump up and turn a summersault in the air before landing on its paws.

Another had a dog that could count. He would tell the dog a certain number and the dog would respond with the same number of barks. Another had a dog for retrieving ducks when he went duck hunting. He said that he would take the dog out in the boat with him and when he shot a duck the dog would jump out of the boat and walk on top of the water and fetch the duck jumping back into the boat. He said he could never teach the dog how to swim.

When these men finished telling their stories then Red Gallagher told about his coon dog and how smart he was. When he was a young fellow they lived not far from the woods and when he wanted a coon hide all he had to do was set a stretch board out on the back step of the house, the dog would look, size it up and take off in the woods and before the end of the day, he would be back with a coon that would fit the stretch board. But he said that one day his mother forgot and set out the ironing board on the back step and the dog hasn't come home yet as he is still looking for a coon to fit that board. We have to keep in mind that these are real life stories.

In his early years Red Gallagher played ball with the famous Springhill Fence Busters who had won the Maritime Championship a number of times. One time when they had played an afternoon game in Truro, N.S. the team went to a restaurant to have their supper. After they had finished their main meal the waitress came to see if they wanted desert. Red ask what kinds was available and was told they had pies and cake. Red then ask the waiter if the pie was the same as his mother made. The waiter assured him that it was, then he said in that case I'll have the cake.

Merrell Murphy and the snow storm (his humor)

Merrell Murphy worked on the main slope of #2 on the back shift (11pm. To 7am.) along with myself and others and I was the relief supervisor. On this particular night there was a sever snow storm leaving several feet of snow by the time we came to the surface at the end of our shift. I knew I wasn't going anywhere until the roads were ploughed as I lived several miles from the mines, but Merrell lived only about a ¼ mile away and always walked to work. I ask him how he was going to get home in the snow that was down and he said he would wait for Fred Nelson who lived a few houses beyond Merrell's, and follow him. To see the humor and get the picture, Fred Nelson who was up in years and was about to retire was given the job of fire-watch on the back shift around the mine property.

Fred was very bowlegged so when Merrell Murphy said he would follow Fred home through the snow he added that the path would be a little narrow at the ankles but that there would be lots of room at the knees.

A lot of years have passed since I have heard some of these stories but they have remained with me and are the reflections of my many years of working in the coal mines. To me it was a wonderful time of working with men who allowed their whit and humor to be a form of pastime while at times working under very difficult circumstances, and no doubt there are many more untold stories that have yet to be heard but sad to say, the majority of those old-timers have now passed away and their stories have been lost forever.

Yes, Springhill has left me with a lot of fond memories that I cherish and that is why I always refer to it as my home town.

Harry Munroe.

A History of Coal Mining
In Springhill

The Springhill Coal Mines were part of what is referred to as the Cumberland Basin Coal Fields.

The first recorded mining in the Cumberland Basin dates back to the early part of the eighteenth century. The General Mining Association had the rights to coal mining in this area. At this time several small production mines were opened by independent operators. In 1879, the General Mining Association grant in Springhill was taken over by the Springhill and Parrsboro Railway Company, which in turn was succeeded by the Cumberland Railway and Coal Company in 1884, and the Dominion Coal Company in 1911.

The Dominion Coal Company continued to work the Springhill coal mines through the 1900's with the last operating mine closing by 1970. A great problem with coal mining at Springhill has been the occurrences of bumps, (that is a bursting of the coal or rock strata under pressure) in the mine levels and long walls. Bumps have occurred over the years in the mines in Springhill, however the #2 mine because of it's dept has had the most significant bumps, with the sever disaster in 1958 in which 76 miners lost their lives.

In the almost 100 years of mining in Springhill, the combined production was 35,345,860 tons of coal according to the N.S. Dept. of Mines records. The coal produced from Springhill Mines was listed as High Volatile. "A" Bituminous Coal with a B.T. U. value of between 11,000 and 13,000, and low ash and sulphur content. (A very good quality coal.)

The seams of coal in Springhill pitched in a North direction starting at approximately 30 degrees and gradually in #2 at the 14,000 foot level being at 22degrees.

The list of coal seams mined and the height of the seams were listed by number, one seam of coal on top of another with a layer of strata sandwiched in between, and the strata was sandstone.

Seams	Average Thickness
No. 1	6 ft.
No. 2	9 ft.
No. 3	8 ft.
No. 4	6 ft.
No. 6	5.6 ft.
No. 7	4 ft.

The original method of mining was what they referred to as Bord and Pillar. A system of coal mining in which the working places are rectangular rooms (bords) off a central road, five or ten times as long as they are broad.

The bords are separated by pillars of solid coal. The pillars were later extracted in retreat mining, letting the roof collapse onto the open space that was created.

During this time horses (some referred to these as pit ponies as they used smaller animals), were used to pull the coal cars, (boxes) along the levels (roadways), to a central location to be hoisted to the surface.

Another method used at that time was called Pulling The Rag. When they were driving a head or tunnel up hill, as the coal was mined the coal was loaded on to a piece of canvas usually by one of the boy miners, (some as young as 10-12 yrs. old), and pulled downhill to a loading chute to loaded into boxes, so their job was called pulling the rag.

When I started working in #1 seam, I first worked with one of those old time workers, Amos Boss who told me that was his first job. He was paid 45 cents a day and in the winter time he said that he would come to work by lantern light and go home the same because you stayed at the work site until the work was completed.

With the advent of compressed air driven machinery, and the depth of the mines, horses were no longer useful for mining in the Springhill mines.

The mining methods then changed to what was referred to as long wall mining. This is referred to as a system of straight coal faces, and in the #2 mine they were 400 ft. long, with approximately 30 miners working the coal face. The coal is mined in a continuous operation, wooden hardwood packs were built to support the roof and as they moved forward new packs were built and the ones behind were re moved., allowing the roof to collapse gradually. I will be describing the long wall method in more detail a little later in my writings.

No. 6&7 Seams were first mined from North Street, a short distance from the Junction Road. During the development stages they mined up under the Junction Road to close to where the school is in order to get the easy coal while also following the seam down in a north direction. This mine operated for a number of years and the mine waste, (stone etc.) can still be seen as you start driving down the connector highway towards SaltSprings.

The coal seams were later reopened through No. 4 mine as a means of keeping all coal handling under one bankhead.

As stated earlier, the Springhill Coal seams pitched at approximately 30 degrees, running in a northerly direction toward Springhill Junction.

No. 1&2 mines used the same main slope for hoisting the coal to the surface (bank head where the coal was weighed and cleaned from any stone, then sorted as to the types, ie. fine, nut, etc.)

The main slope for No. 2 when I started working in the early 1940's went down to the 7100 ft. main bottom where the empty rakes (16 boxes), were lowered and the full rake (loaded boxes) were hoisted to the surface. The main slope was doubled tract halfway down so that you would have full boxes being hoisted while empty ones were being lowered at the same time.

Method of supporting the roof of the slopes. As time passed most of the main slope of No. 2 was steel arched, with the remainder of the slope supported with steel booms, that is railway rails with plank lagging overhead to support the roof and these steel booms were supported on both ends with spruce props. These booms were about 2 feet apart. The same method was used on No. 4 main and back slopes as well as the main bottoms at the 7800 in No. 2 and the 3300 bottom in No. 4.

The main bottoms extended westward for 500ft. to allow room for the full and empty coal boxes, it being double tract also, the full boxes on the low side and the empty ones on the high side.

The back slope was an extension of the main slope by means of the main bottom, was single tract, and just prior to the bump in 1958, had extended down to the 15000 ft. dept.

In the early 1950's the main bottom was extended down to the 7800 ft. level in No. 2 to allow for further development. Ventilation was very important in the mining process so that the methane gas that is released from the coal as it is being mined can be diluted to the point of not being dangerous.

In the mine development, the fan slope was on the east side of the main slope, approximately 100 ft. apart. A large surface fan was used to force air into the mine. At the 3300 ft. level there was a tunnel to No. 4 as an emergency escape for the miners in case the main slope was blocked off. This tunnel was used during the 1956 explosion in No.4 to rescue those miners that were trapped.

No. 2 fan way slope extended down to the 7400ft. level, where a booster fan forced air to the bottom of the mine. At this level the fan way crossed over the back slope and went down on the west side of the back slope through the pipe board which also housed the compressed air pipe line as well as the water line used to pump the water out of the mine. Both of these pipelines went to the bottom of the mines and there was a number of pumping stations along the way so that the water could reach the surface to be discharged, as the mine was continually making water. The return air would flow through the long walls and up the main slope to the surface.

When the long wall system was developed first in No. 1&2 mines, the levels (roadways) were driven in approximately 2 miles, both east and west of the main slop and each level in No.2 were 400 ft. apart and in No. 1 300 ft. apart and it was referred as the retreat method, that is they would start at the end of the levels and work their way back to the slope, removing the coal as they retreated. At the entrance of the level next to the slope there was a double drum air haulage for moving the coal boxes on what was called a trip made up of 32 boxes and these would be loaded at the bottom of the long wall. As stated earlier, the long wall was 400 ft. long, and there was two sets of shaker pans that were driven in an up and down motion by long wall air engines and the pans were v shaped to keep the coal in them, and a loading chute on the level for loading the boxes.

In No. 2 on the west side of the main slope, just below the 6000 ft. level the coal was not mined as they began to encounter sever bumps, only the pipe slope was developed. From there on No. 2 only mined the coal on the east side of the main and back slopes. When I started working in the mines in the early 40's, I was assigned to the 10,200 long wall. There were three long walls in operation at that time, which meant that a stretch of 1200 ft. was being mined at the same time, and the walls were staggered, that is each wall was about 200ft. apart. Day and afternoon shifts (7-3 & 3-11), were production shifts, and maintenance as well as shifting the pans was carried as required on the back shift (11-7).

In No. 2 coal was mined by hand, that is with a hand pick and shovel and a chipper pick when the coal was hard. Under normal circumstances, it would take the miners two days (for both shifts) to clean off the wall, a strip approximately 9 ft. wide and prepare it for a shift of pans, again next to the coal face. This was an ongoing process on all three long walls.

As the coal was mined, props and packs were installed and built to support the roof of the mine. The props were of spruce poles approximately 6 inches on the small end and the packs were made of hardwood 8x6 inches by 6 ft. long, built with two pieces across and two pieces up and down much like a log house, built from the floor of the mine to the roof. There was usually two lines of packs the length of the wall about 20 ft. apart, and as the coal was being mined, new lines of packs were built and the back line was removed which allowed the waste roof to fall behind them. The pans were shifted and the packs were removed on the back shift.

During the mining process as the coal was being removed small bumps would occur from time to time, it would shake things up, the air would be full of coal dust, and the props and packs would creak and crack, and after a while the air would clear, and everyone would go back to work. I had that experience a number of times.

In the spring of 1958 it was managements decision to have all three long walls brought in line with each other rather than stagger them as was done in the past. The older experienced miners warned management of the danger but the warning went unheeded and many miners became nervous about going to work, and if a bump was to occur they hoped that it would be at a time when the mine was idle.

On Thursday, Oct. 23, 1858, the older miners prediction came true, claiming 76 lives. Following the rescue of the survivors and recovery of the bodies, the machinery and equipment was removed from the mines, and it was then sealed permanently, thus ending Dosco's operation in Springhill.

I started working in No. 2 when I was 16yrs. old and when I was 18 yrs. old I joined the R.C.A.F. for approximately two years and then returned to Springhill to again work in the mines as I had coal dust in my veins so to speak.

When I returned to the mines I was assigned to work in No. 1. I studied coal mining and became a shot fire, that is, I was qualified to blast the coal which was the method used in both No. 1&4 mines.

By the early 1950's the C.N. railway was switching from coal fired steam engines to diesel and they were the major user of Springhill coal so things were beginning to slow down in the coal mining industry. The last long wall coal mining in No. 1 was at the 5700 ft. level and there was no new development work being done which indicated it was coming to an end.

Shortly before that a stone tunnel was started at the 5700 ft. level to go into no. 3 coal seam which would have added new life to the mining industry in Springhill. I was one of the shot fires working on this project but it was never completed due to the bleak outlook of the coal mining industry at that time. I was then transferred to overseeing the maintenance on the main slope of No. 2 on the back shift.

Method of mining in No. 1 seam. The long wall method was used and these walls were 300ft. long and they had two walls going at the same time on opposite shifts, day and afternoon, changing week about. The seams used a Samson cutting machine, like a large chain saw, with a 6 ft. jib, and it would cut a swath 8 inches thick, at a height of 3 ft. of the payment, the length of the long wall, so that the coal could be blasted with monovalve blasting powder, because it was a harder coal. The miners had their own space of about 20 ft. and when their block of coal was removed they could go home.

The Samson machine was driven by compressed air and had a cable to pull it along as it was used to cut uphill. There is a sample of a Sampson cutting machine at the Miner's Museum in Springhill. The shaker pans in these long walls were shifted after each production shift.

No. 4, and 6&7 seams used the same mining methods as No. 1

The outcropping of no. 4 seam was in the Rodger field at the upper end of Morris Street but in order to have the coal from this seam processed at the same bank head as No. 1&2 the hoisting slope was driven on an angle through 3300 ft. of stone to reach the coal at the 3300 ft. level where they developed their main bottom and from there drove their back slope and the long walls off it. Their main bottom was similar to that of no. 2

As a point of interest at the time of the explosion in 1956, Lee Blinhhorn who was one of the hoisting engineers on the back slope of no. 4, traded shifts with Jack Ward and thus avoided the explosion. Lee never went into the mines again, moved to Dartmouth and worked at the Nova Scotia Power Plant on water street in Halifax until his retirement.

No. 6 & 7 seams was entered through No. 4 back slope around the 5000 ft level. Mining of these seams came to an end when No. 4 closed following the explosion in 1956. These seams also used the Samson cutting machine in their method of mining.

No. 4 mine began to electrify some of it's equipment prior to the explosion and it was when a rake of coal broke away on the back slope and severed the electric cable, thus causing an arching or flame setting of a dust and gas explosion. 39 lives were lost as a result of this and when the rescue work was completed of those considered alive the mine was sealed due to the fear of another explosion. The mine was reopened in Jan. 1957 to recover the remaining bodies, and then the mine was sealed for good.

I was involver in the rescue work during both disasters. In the No. 4 explosion I worked as a Draegerman and in No. 2, first as a Draegerman and when the ventilation system was back in operation and the gas was cleared The Draegermen were no longer required then I volunteered to work as a barefaced miner in the recovery of all the bodies.

As a 4th. Generation coal miner, mining had been an important part of my early life so I have written this account from my mind's eye while my mind is still reality good.

There were many brave men who risked their lives during these two disasters to try and help their fellow workers and they deserve a lot of credit.

During those years of coal mining in Springhill, the mines claimed 424 lives and when you think of it, what a terrible cost, but at the time it was an acceptable way of life.

Springhill's Connection With The Moose River Gold Mine Disaster 1936

On Easter Sunday, April 12, 1936 at 11 PM., three men entered the gold mine at Moose River, (Dr. David Robertson, Alf. Scadding, and Herman Magill), a cave in followed on the entrance slope trapping them underground and as they say, the rest became history.

Brave men from a number of mining communities arrived at the Moose River mine site to assist in the rescue operation that lasted for ten days, including those miners from Springhill.

When you visit the Miners Museum on the Black River Road in Springhill, N.S., and as you are about to leave the Museum to tour the underground mine, on the right side of the building next to the door you will see a picture of some of the rescue workers from Springhill, and also a picture of Billy Bell the diamond driller.

Of the rescue workers pictured are Frank Stevens, leading the team as well as Jim Rushton, George Terris, Duncan McNeil, these were men I knew as well as others listed on the photo. As a point of interest Frank Stevens was in charge of the draegermen during the Mine disasters in 1956 & 1958. He was a real team leader in whom the draegermen had a lot of respect.

Jim Rushton is credited with bringing out Alf. Scadding, carrying him out on his back and after that he and Duncan McNeil re-entered the mine to bring out the body of Herman Magill who had died on the seventh day of their being trapped in the gold mines.

Billy Bell at that time was doing some drilling for the Dept, of mines, his headquarters was in New Glasgow, and he was sent to the mine site in Moose River with his crew of men to see if they could be of any assistance.

On arrival at the site he took an educated guess as to where and at what angle to start drilling to try and make contact with the trapped men.

By this time many had given up hope that the trapped men were still alive., The diamond drill broke through at the 141 ft. level on Sat. the 18th, and several attempts were made to try and contact the trapped men, and finally Billy Bell ask for a small whistle that would fit into the one and a half inch bore hole, connected to a compressed air line and by this means he was able to make contact with the men on Sunday Apr. 19th. At 12:30 A.M. (approx. seven days from when the ordeal began.)

Liquids, candles, and a small microphone was lowered through the bore hole. The total ordeal lasted for 10 days.

Following the completion of the rescue operations, the shafts were sealed.

In 1986, on the 50th. Anniversary of the Moose River Gold Mine disaster the site was turned into a park with a stone cairn encasing the diamond drill casing from Billy Bell's diamond drill hole.

At that official opening in 1986, Billy bell was presented with a plaque with the steam whistle mounted on it for his successful efforts during the rescue operation. That plaque still hangs on the wall in the Bell house on Elm St., in Springhill, and I have visited the park at Moose River a number of times. We Springhiller's always referred to him as Billy Bell the diamond driller. Some years ago someone gave me a copy of a poem about Billy Bell, and his Involvement in the rescue called "Ode To Billy Bell." With the initials J.A.H. 77. The writer is now unknown.

This poem aptly describes the effort of all those brave men who risked their lives to try and rescue their fellow man and of the efforts of Billy Bell.

On another note, Wilf Carter, Canada' singing and yodeling cowboy was singing over CBS New York, at that time and his brother Lovet was visiting him also at that time, and a number of years ago while he was still alive I ask him how Wilf Carter came to write and record the song, "Rescue at Moose River." Lovet told me that as reports would come in on the radio describing each days events, then Wilf would add another verse to the song and 12 hours after the rescue was completed he went into the recording studio and had it recorded. Wilf Carter was a prolific song writer having written over 600 songs during his career.

So the Moose River Gold Mines rescue operation was just another part of the role that Springhill miners played in the history of mining in Nova Scotia, always ready to come to the aid of their comrade in need. Even though mining is now a thing of the past, may we in Springhill never forget that rich history.

"Ode To Billy Bell"

On easter sunday in thirty-six
At eleven o'clock that night
A shaft at the moose river mine caved in
And bottled three men up tight,

Trapped one hundred and forty feet down
They stared in horror and shock
At their only exit tightly sealed
By tons of fallen rock.

Above, the ground just opened and sank
When the roof collapsed in the mine
And the cable house gave a mighty heave
As the air pipes burst with a whine.

There was, just then, no way to tell
If the three were alive or dead
But rescuers came from near and far
Their hopes outweighing their dread,

The men in the shaft shivered with cold
As black, icy water rained down
Death by exposure or starving seemed sure
If first they did not drown.

But searching around with their oil lamps
They found a dry wooden box
And set it alight with ten-dollar bills;
Could smoke escape the rocks?

Get through those rocks and rubble it did
And curl its way out of the ground
To be seen with joy on the monday a.m.
As the cry "they're alive" went around.

By that afternoon two derelict shafts
Were being cleared of fill,
While a vertical hole was also begun
With dynamite blast and drill.

Meanwhile-down in the shaft below
The three men heated stones
To hold against their freezing flesh
And ease their aching bones.

When at last the fire went out
They huddled closer for heat
Fearful of the water pouring in
And swirling around their feet.

From westville, springhill, stellarton too,
Still their rescuers came
Three hundred in all from miles around
They sought no money or fame.

Despite their numbers, their courage and skill
The progress made monday was slow
In one of the shafts they met solid rock
On tuesday the other collapsed below.

But to those imprisoned in the shaft
The sounds of rescue gave hope
Although they feared another fall
Of the rock trapped up the slope.

Thinking that they too might be heard
They began on some pipes to pound

Harry E. Munroe

Straining their ears for answering raps
But there never came back a sound.

By wednesday only the vertical hole
Showed signs of the progress made
But even that was a mere thirty feet
And hopes were beginning to fade.

The wives of the men cried unashamed
As they stood by the pit that day
They knew that the hole was a "death shaft"
Not one would get out alive that way.

With time running out, those in command
Called for a diamond drill crew
As it had to be known if the three still lived
And a big number ten might get through.

At dawn on thursday the crew arrived
After driving through the night
Since easter monday the man in charge
Had been begging to join the fight.

He was lean, laconic and thirty-three
A miners man you could tell
Who both smoked and chewed his tabbaco
And his name was - billy bell.

Billy worked out of new glasgow
Though springhill was really his town
He knew how it felt to be trapped below
And vowed to get the drill down.

Scouting the site with an engineer
He was asked to sink the drill
On an angle down to the shaft below
A job needing guts and skill.

Without mine charts of the workings
It would be like a shot in the dark
But billy pushed up the peak of his hat
And began to locate his mark.

Finally, on firm ground off to one side
His assistants helped him make ready
The three-ton, air-powered drilling rig
A monster that had to stand steady.

When all was set billy angled the drill
At sixty-two degrees
Spat once for luck then began his work
In the face of an icy breeze.

For twenty-four hours he drove that drill
Without a wink of sleep
Through sixty feet of quartz and slate
Seeking those three in the deep.

And they could hear the sound of the drill
Like distant machine gun fire
But their foodless bodies wracked with pain
Were fast beginning to tire,

Lying in darkness, their lights burned out
They shook with fear and cold
Listening to the sounds from up above
And praying their strength would hold.

In the so called "death shaft" overhead
The work went on in shifts
As more volunteers kept coming in
To add their precious gifts.

But none gave more than billy bell
Who kept at it night and day

Braving the rain, the wind and the snow
Drilling and feeling his way.

So sensitive was his feel for the rig
That without the need of sight
Just by the vibrations in his hands
He knew what the drill would bite.

Each time the bit sank ten more feet
Billy's crew would haul it out
Then turn on another ten foot length
They knew what they were about,

As friday passed and saturday came
The headlines that morning were grim
"abandon hope of saving men..."
But billy bell wouldn't give in.

Twice in his life time - once as a boy
He'd been rescued from a pit
So, remembering, billy pushed himself
And that diamond studded bit.

To some it seemed that he was clothed
With a kind of queer devotion
But the man just kept on doing his job
And ignoring all the commotion.

At noon that saturday billy's drill
Broke through into the shaft
His "shot in the dark" a bulls eye
A mark of that man and his craft.

The miners expectantly gathered around
As billy uncoupled the drill
From the slender pipe it left in the ground
Then, suddenly all was still.

Kneeling over the mouth of the casing
Billy let go with a shout
But the only sound coming back to his ear
Was that of the water rushing about.

Next they dropped a railway flare
And then a thin pen-light
But still no response from down below
It seemed they had lost the fight,

Unbeknown to billy and his friends
The flare had ignited below
But behind a pile of rock and wood
Where it blazed with a livid glow,

Thinking a fire was beginning to start
One of the three limped about
Splashing water on the hidden flare
Until it fizzled out.

By nine p.m. all hope was gone
The three it seemed were dead
But billy refused to leave the site
And sent for a whistle instead.

Attaching it to his drilling rod
In place of the diamond bit
He lowered the small steam whistle
Down the casing into the pit,

Then, using a chugging compressor
And forgetting his need to sleep
He kept on blowing air down the pipe
So the whistle would sound in the deep,

For hours it did no more than hiss
But when at last it blew

One of the three began to search
And finally found the clue.

It was just after midnight on sunday
As billy was checking his gear
That there suddenly came a rap on the pipe
"my god", he yelled, "they're here"

Pounding back he cleared the tube
"hello there", said a voice,
One was ill but all were alive
Good reason to rejoice,

The wives were next to kneel in the mud
And call down to their men
Grateful to hear their voices once more
But the fight wasn't over then.

Down the pipe went candles and matches
And slender vials of brandy
Things like coffee, a one way phone
And bits of chocolate candy,

But time was running out for the three
The water was rising, one cried
And then on monday without a sound
The one with pneumonia died.

About that time the men on top
Reopened an other old shaft
A long-shot for sure and dangerous
This try would be their last.

The shaft was really a suicide tunnel
Yet miners stood in line
To take their turn and give their all
For those still alive in the mine.

For two more days without a pause
They chipped and hacked their way
Through a tangle of debris and rock
To where the survivors lay.

At eleven-forty on wednesday night
The rescuers reached the two
And brought them up from out of the deep
Their ten days of hell were through.

Carried between the lines of friends
Who cheered and jumped around
The two men weakly gave their thanks
For rescue from the ground,

Then came silence for the one who died
As his body was gently brought out
The only sound being that of his dog
Who whimpered and wandered about.

And so it was that two of three
Were saved from a dismal pit
As hundreds of nova scotian men
Stepped in to do their bit,

Among them a man called billy bell
The persistent diamond driller
Who guided his drill with guts and skill
Like a helmsman at the tiller.

He was the one who would not quit
When others were filled with dread
And believing the three could never survive
Had given them up for dead.

But, modest as well as tenacious,
He later admitted his fears

"blind luck - i couldn't do it again
If i tried for a hundred years."

So, if ever you visit moose river
A small cairn and casing will tell
Of the ten day fight to save three lives
By some men and one billy bell.

J.A.H. '77

About the writer.

I was born in a farmhouse on the Gulf Shore, below Pugwash, the 3rd. of 6 children in our family on March 8, 1928. My mother was a school teacher from Springhill, who was teaching in the country when she met my father and when I was one year old they moved to Springhill as on my mother's side they were coal miners and they thought that our family would have a better quality of life by moving there with my father working in the mines. In my early years while growing up, my father never talked about his work in the mines but I spent a lot of time around my grandfather who was in charge of the ventilation at the mines and on Saturday afternoons some of the men who worked with him would gather at his house to enjoy a glass of beer and talk about what was happening at the mines and I would listen with keen interest and it helped me to develop a desire to become a miner.

We were brought up during the hungry thirties, money was scarce, there was no such thing as getting an allowance from your parents, so we were anxious to have money to spend which meant going to work.

In order to work in the mines you had to be 16 years old so at 15 years of age I started working at the Springhill Dairy with the agreement with my mother that I would go to night school to finish my education. It was a job that paid $3.00 a day, seven days a week. The day started at 6:30 AM, and you worked until all the milk was processed and the equipment was cleaned and ready for the next day.

At age 16 I reached my goal of working in the coal mines. I was getting $3.74 a day with weekends off.

At age 18 I enlisted in the RCAF, my home base was Edmonton, Alberta. I was with the North West Command, as a heavy equipment operator. I spent two winters in the North clearing runways. But the call of returning to the coal mines was too strong to keep me away so I received my discharge from the Air Force and went back to the Springhill coal mines.

On returning I started going to night school to study Mining and attained my Mine Examiner & Shot Fire's papers. As time passed I realized that coal mining in Springhill was coming to an end so I started back to night school studying Stationary Engineering and by the time the mines closed following the 1958 disaster I had obtained my 3rd. class certificate and had the offer of three different jobs, so I choose to work at the Dorchester Penitentiary in the boiler room, and that would allow me to remain in Springhill, while driving back and forwards to work.

I continued my studies in Stationary Engineering through correspondence and eventually obtained my 1st. class papers, and when Springhill Institution was built I was appointed as the Chief Engineer.

After that I studied Mechanical Drafting and obtained my certificate in that trade. In 1971 I was appointed as the Plant Superintendent at the Springhill Institution, a position I held until I retired, and I also taught Stationary Engineering at night school for a number of years.

In those days the Springhill High school night classes made it a bee hive of activity five nights a week offering many courses and trades. This was the forerunner of trade schools later to be called Vocational Schools/ Community Colleges.

In conclusion, I must say that Springhill has always been good to me, leaving me with many fond memories.

Harry Munroe.

A collection of some of my memorabilia

My check number For getting your Underground lamp And pay.

The Carnegie Ribbon is a memento Of the Carnegie Plaque presented to Springhill for the men who risked their Lives in the rescue work underground. Oct. 23- to Nov. 2, 1958.

Mine Rescue Pin These were given To the Draegermen.

This is a picture of when No. 3 mine was in operation. In the foreground you can see the huge air fan which was used to pump fresh air into the working area of the mine and the return air came up the main slope to the surface thus carrying away the methane gas that was released as the coal was being mined. Behind that is seen the elevated bank head where the coal is brought to the surface, dumped and sorted. As seen by the smoke stacks, all machinery at that time was run by steam and compressed air. Later on the mine was flooded because of a fire and never reopened. In the early 1950's a tunnel was started from the 5700 of the main slope of No 2 main slope in which I was one of the shot fires (blasting the stone), but after going a short distance was abandoned due to slumping coal sales.

Picture provided by Kenneth Langille.

Town of Springhill, N. S.

Pictures From The Past

This picture is from the left side of main street as you go down. The first building which was just below the Miner's Hall (now the library), is no longer in existence.

The next three buildings still remain and are in use. The other buildings, including the post office building showing the clock were destroyed in the main street fire in the 1950's. Below that is the ball park and race track, and then the smoke stacks from the buildings at the Coal Mine site.

In conclusion, I will always reflect on the words written by James B. Brown in his book Miracle Town, Springhill, N.S.

James was a friend of mine and we had many conversations together regarding mining.

His quote was: The complete history of Springhill can not be captured in a single book, in a single lifetime, and quite possibly never on paper.

However, there is still much to tell, still many years to survive and hopefully a story-teller to continue where this writing ends for a great man once said for the world to hear. "There will always be a Springhill."

Harry Munroe.

Printed in the United States
By Bookmasters